Divine Reality

DIVINE REALITY

When Mere Truth Becomes Reality

RUDI SWANEPOEL

Essence
PUBLISHING

Belleville, Ontario, Canada

Divine Reality

Copyright © 2001, Rudi Swanepoel

ISBN: 1-55306-234-5

Essence Publishing is a Christian Book Publisher dedicated to furthering the work of Christ through the written word. For more information, contact: 44 Moira Street West, Belleville, Ontario, Canada K8P 1S3.
Phone: 1-800-238-6376. Fax: (613) 962-3055.
E-mail: info@essencegroup.com
Internet: www.essencegroup.com

Printed in Canada
by

With Deepest Appreciation

To my lovely wife, Sharon, who will always be my better half. Thank you for making our married years the best of my life! Your adventurous spirit and loving heart has kept us on the cutting edge of ministry—exactly where the Lord wants us to be. Thank you for the great times together, both in God's Presence and each other's. You have always played a prominent role in the ministry God gave us to reveal the realm of Divine Reality. I have attempted to put in words what we have searched for, discovered, and lived together. I love you, always!

Table of Contents

Foreword

There are few men whose preaching and teaching have impacted our lives as that of Rudi Swanepoel. We met Rudi and his lovely wife, Sharon, a few years ago when they dropped into one of our Sunday evening services. A few weeks later we asked them to share in an evening worship service—and oh, what a glorious time it was! The "Glory of the Lord" filled the church and we found ourselves worshiping in a manner we had never before encountered. That evening began a special relationship with the Swanepoels, which to this day continues to grow.

We believe it is important for you to know the author of this book on "Divine Reality" a little better. Rudi Swanepoel is a man with a great anointing on his life. He is a special young man of God who has, through his presentation of the Word of God and his life example, shown himself to be the "Real Deal." I have often said, with regard to Rudi, "what you see is who he is:" focused—sincere—always joyful; an encourager to the "nth" degree. Rudi Swanepoel is just plain REAL!

So what does the "real man of God" give as a title to his first book? *Divine Reality*. As we thought about his work, we began to understand that this book is not only about how we all should live, but how Rudi and Sharon live their lives, themselves.

We believe as you read this wonderful book, you will experience a blessing. As you encounter the scriptural portrayal of Gideon coming to life, it will provide you with insights into daily divine living and a desire to press more deeply into the things of God. Rudi's beautiful use of illustrations from his own life experiences will allow you to adapt the relevancy of the message into your life.

I pray you receive that which is written herein with an openness that allows you to encounter the fullness of what God desires to do in your life. May you find yourself hungering for more of God and for a life of "Divine Reality."

—*Rev. Bill and Lynna Roberts,*
Christ Chapel, Woodbridge, Virginia

Introduction

As a boy on a farm called Missgunst, in South Africa, I had my first lesson on the Reality of God. Just like all young boys, I could not wait for the holidays to start so we could go to the farm. We stayed in the city, but the farm was so much fun, with lots of great things to do. One of my favorites was to get on one of the huge tractors, crank up the engine, and drive it around the big old farmyard, much to the disgust of the chickens and other livestock.

"Stay away from the bees!" my dad's voice echoed through the house every day. "Believe me, you do not want to be stung by them." I knew my dad told the truth, but somehow, the truth of the sting of a bee never really got through to me until the hot summer day when I drove the tractor across the wide plains of the yard, disturbing the peace of every living creature, including the honeybees in a nearby hive.

"Ouch! It hurts and burns like fire!" I cried. Dad was right—I did not want to be stung. The pain of the sting moved me much faster than the words of caution from my dad. Why didn't I listen? It seemed my personal close encounter with a swarm of bees weighed much more than the truth spoken by my loving earthly father. Meeting the bees changed my life. I soon carried evidence of the reality of a bee-sting: my eye was swollen shut for everyone to see. Every time I looked at myself in the mirror, or when a friend reminded me of my eye, or someone laughed at the swelling, I was confronted by my newfound reality. That day changed my thoughts about bees forever! The truth about bees became a reality in my life.

Ever since that day, God started showing me the difference between mere truth and reality. The Bible is filled with truths and promises; yet, when we look at the lives of Christians, many believe in the truth of each promise, but not all promises become reality to them.

You will know the Truth and the Truth will set you free (John 8:32). It is not about knowing facts and gathering information, but in experiencing the Truth Himself: Jesus Christ. He *is the Way and the Truth and the Life* (John 14:6). Christians know all about Him, but few really know Him. The Truth must become a reality in our lives—like the bees on that farm in South Africa. When the Reality of God broke through in my spirit, it changed my life forever. I carried, and carry, the evidence of the Divine Reality in me much like my swollen eye; people started to see a difference in me. They saw a change. It changed my thoughts, my life and even my body. The light of God started to shine through me for others to see and enjoy.

In this book I want to bring you closer and deeper into a new relationship with Jesus and present Him as the reality you cannot live without. I am going to use the practicality of the Word of God to highlight God's principles of living in the Divine Reality. We will look into the life of Gideon, God's chosen warrior, who was one day thrust into a new dimension of the Reality of God. My two-fold prayer is that your life will be changed through the discovery of the Divine Reality in your life and that this book will help you get there.

This is not a book based on theological statements and principles, but rather a sharing of my heart. In the process of change, I broke through in a discovery of the Reality of God.

—*Rudi Swanepoel*

The Reality of Your Situation

*A*nd the hand of Midian prevailed against Israel.
Because of Midian the Israelites made themselves the
dens which are in the mountains and the caves and the
strongholds. For whenever Israel had sown their seed, the
Midianites and Amalekites and the people of the east came
up against them. They would encamp against them and
destroy their crops as far as Gaza and leave no nourish-
ment for Israel.... And Israel was greatly impoverished
because of the Midianites, and the Israelites cried to the
Lord (Judges 6:2-4,6).

The Midianites pestered and tormented the people of
God for seven years. They chased the people of Israel into

15

the mountains and the once-great nation of God was forced by an enemy to hide away. The Midianites stopped at nothing. As time went by, they invented more hideous ways to make life miserable for Israel. Slowly but surely, they squashed the very life out of Israel until all that was left was nothing more than a memory of days gone by, when God did mighty deeds among them. Days that seemed so far away because of their present circumstances. They were greatly impoverished by the enemy.

Life With the Enemy in Your Back Yard

Israel made adjustments in their way of life. They had to be more careful with their crops. They had to find better ways of dealing with poverty and daily survival. It is remarkable to see how well the people of God coped with an enemy in their backyard. The reality of their situation became a measuring stick by which they measured life. Everything, including the things of God, had to fit into that reality. They were so consumed by things happening around them that they lost the reality of being the people of the Only Living God Who loved them.

The Church, as a whole, finds herself in the same predicament as Israel. Christians who once were on fire for God made adjustments in their lives because of an enemy and circumstances surrounding them. In many ways, we have traded our victorious way of living for a slave-like mentality and have become content with living under a burden of fear, doubt, and uncertainty. All we have left is a blessed memory of a distant past where God did something great in our lives, or a past move of God, but even the memory of that is blurred by the reality of our situation. Can you identify with this? How do *you* fit into this picture?

Maybe you once had a vision from God for your life—but now you are hopelessly entangled in the frustrations of living Christian-like to please others. You find it difficult to know what God is doing, saying, or wanting for you today. Maybe you have traded your personal experience with God for an empty knowledge of Him. Truth, without the reality behind it, makes for an empty life filled with frustrations and disappointments.

Have you lost joy that once was the source of your strength? Did you have to make many adjustments in your life? It really is remarkable how you cope with these kinds of situations. On the outside, people would never know that you are having a tough time. You can hide your frustrations with a smile and a "God bless you."

Everything you do is measured by the reality you live in. Every plan, idea, and purpose must fit into your current situation and must have the enemy's stamp of approval on it! Your life is governed by the external, natural look of things, and not by the deeper spiritual reality activated by faith. Smith Wigglesworth, also called the Apostle of Faith, once said: "I am not moved by what I see, but by what I believe." Today, many Christians—people just like you and me— have adopted the opposite way of life. They are not moved by their faith anymore, but by what they see in the natural. They are imprisoned by the reality of their situation.

During the Christmas season, the truth of Christ in the manger, the Baby Messiah who came to this world, is evident. In every mall, virtually around every corner, Nativity scenes add to the atmosphere of Christmas, helping stores sell more stuff. The reality of His coming, leaving the splendor of heaven and the comfort of His throne for a nasty stable and cruel world, seldom dawns on us. In fact, this reality should be a driving force in us every day —not just in December.

On Easter Sunday we rejoice because of the victory of Christ on the cross and overcoming the grave—but it should be a burning reality in us while we face every situation each day of our lives.

Every time we partake in Holy Communion, we should be stirred inside—not because of a mere truth written in 1 Corinthians 11, but by the reality of the meaning of the sacrament; how we become one with the One Whose body was broken, Whose blood was spilled, Who paid the ultimate and high price for our sin so we could be saved.

In everything we do, there is a bigger, greater reality that surpasses any situation. It is bigger than any enemy. In reading your Bible, praying your prayers, going to work or relaxing at home, in having fun with a few friends, or pressing through tough times, there is a Divine Reality guiding you and keeping you in constant victory.

A Bigger Reality

The fact is, friend, you are not called to *be* history, but rather to *make* it. You do not have to live a life of mere existence. You can rise above anything the world throws at you. Stop being a product of your circumstances. Let the things that surround you be a product of your victorious life. Do not let the devil write defeat all over you—do some writing yourself! Winners cannot be losers at the same time. Do not put this book down just yet. Let me show you how to live this great life.

Food for thought:

- You are not called to be a product of your circumstances.
- You can rise above your situation and see the Bigger Picture, just like the Lord sees it!
- A life of constant victory means the absence of defeat.

The Divine Reality

Now the Angel of the Lord came and sat under the oak at Ophrah, which belonged to Joash the Abiezrite, and his son Gideon was beating wheat in the winepress to hide it from the Midianites (Judges 6:11).

Yes, there is an enemy. Yes, he wants to destroy you. Yes, sometimes just like Gideon, you are forced to hide away and adjust your life because of this enemy. And yes, there is an unseen Presence seated in your life very near to you. This is the very promise that kept the people of God going through all ages. Abraham left all to follow this Unseen Presence. He did not even know where the Lord was taking him, but he did not think twice even though he knew in the natural he could lose everything. Why?

Moses, a castaway, a murderer, knew he would never be able to go back to his people in Egypt. He knew he was wanted for murder—yet he went back to the very king who would not hesitate to kill him. Why?

Why didn't Daniel, when his circumstances changed and people turned against him, adjust his life because of his enemies? How could Paul, Peter, and all the other great men of God press on relentlessly and in victory amidst trouble, trial, and tribulation?

The answer to all of these questions is the same. They lived according to a Divine Reality, where nothing in the world could match the reality about God in them. They lived it, breathed it, ate it, preached with it, witnessed by it, and performed miracles because of it. It was the reality of the very presence of the Living God—the realization that the Creator of all things is closer than a breath away. Yet, they did not just start living the way they did. Each one of them had to learn how to live and grow into a life in the Divine Reality.

Frightened and Intimidated

When we look at Gideon, we see a poor, frightened young man hiding from the enemy. He managed to save a few straws of wheat, but because of the situation he was in, he was forced to thresh the wheat in a winepress. Normally he would never even think to beat wheat in the winepress, but he adapted wonderfully. The reality of his situation forced him to live a life of mere existence—surviving one day to another. He was totally unaware of the Angel (God in Person) with him. He was so blinded by things in the natural that he could not see the bigger picture.

There are so many poor, frightened young Christians, just like Gideon. Defeated, ruined, and full of anger because of all the mishaps in life. Remember, Gideon had nothing to do with the situation he was in. He did not bring it on himself and he could not change it by himself. He was caught, trapped, and he wanted out. Today, so many people want out, but their own efforts are in vain.

Another Hiding Place

Gideon had to exchange his hiding place (winepress) for another. *He who dwells in the secret place of the Most High shall remain stable and fixed under the shadow of the Almighty [Whose power no foe can withstand]* (Psalm 91:1). There is another hiding place that you can go to: the secret place of the Most High. Because it is a secret place, the enemy does not know where it is or how to get there. It is in the presence of the Almighty, where everything grows dim and seems insignificant. The only thing that one is aware of is the very presence of the Lord and the awesome power that attracts you to Him. It is the power of His everlasting, unfailing love that cannot be understood outside of the secret place.

The Apostle Paul urged us to *Walk and live in the Spirit* (Galatians 5:25). To *Imitate me just as I also imitate Christ* (1 Corinthians 11:1, NKJV). He found the secret place and nothing could derail or distract him again—not the worst chains and jailhouses, nor the agonizing humiliation brought over him by his once-close friends, the Pharisees. He had to go through more in the natural than most of us will ever have to endure, but he kept getting stronger and happier. He found joy in the Reality of God. He found peace and wisdom. He found life.

Holy Citizenship

But we are citizens of the state (commonwealth, homeland) which is in heaven (Philippians 3:20). As a citizen of a country, you have the right to live in that country, and you are protected by the laws of that country. If you visit another country, you need a passport and a visa which must be renewed from time to time. There is a song that says: "We are strangers, we are aliens. We are not of this world." Many Christians are strangers and aliens in their homeland, the secret place of the Most High. They spend so much time in the natural realm that it has become *the* only reality to them. They trade their place in the Spirit Realm for a materialistic, natural life dictated by circumstance.

Stop beating wheat in the winepress! Stop jamming Scripture verses into the context of your situation. You can quote verse after verse in the natural until you are blue in the face—and the only change will be the color of your face. It will not take care of the enemy. It will not change your attitude. It will not change your circumstances. But when you speak the verse, activated by the Divine Reality rising up inside of you, it comes alive with the power of God and it will change you! Maybe you feel alone. Maybe you do not see God close to you. Know He is there, right now, sitting under the oak tree near the winepress where you're hiding away! Gideon did not know it right then, but his life was about to be changed—never to be the same again! God gave him a Reality Check.

Food for Thought:

- In the presence of an enemy, look for the Oak.
- Fear forces you to take extreme measures, doing strange things in strange places.
- What is bigger: God or your circumstances?

Reality Check

A nd the Angel of the Lord appeared to him and said
to him, "The Lord is with you, you mighty man of
[fearless] courage" (Judges 6:12).

Would you like to see God face-to-face? How about
seeing an angel? All of us would really like to see at least
an angel sometime. "If God would only send Gabriel to tell
me something. I really need direction. I want to hear the
voice of God." I remember these words rolling over my lips
many times in despair. At times I was so consumed by what
was happening to me in the natural. If only I could see past
my own situation. Well, it happened!

No, an angel did not appear to me to tell me what I needed to hear—although I am still open to such an encounter. The Lord appeared or manifested His presence to me in a very real and wonderful way. Like Gideon, who was unaware of the presence of the Angel of the Lord sitting under the oak nearby, I was unaware of God's presence in every situation I found myself in. Now I realize that He was always so close, but it did not seem evident at the time. It took a manifestation of the tangible presence of the Lord to catch my attention. At first I did not realize what was going on, but God took my attention off my problems and situations and I focused in on His presence. The Unseen Presence changed to a tangible awareness of God.

A Great Start

After our marriage, Sharon and I went to Bloemfontein, a city in the heart of sunny South Africa. We were placed at a church in the southern suburbs of the city, to start out in the ministry as associate pastors. People referred to our church as the "Cross-Church," because of a 90-foot-high tower with a huge cross on top overlooking the city. It was a wonderful time in our lives. The church grew in three years from 500 to 1,000 people! We were five dedicated pastor-couples who wanted to see God working in the lives of people. We saw many people saved, delivered, and healed by the power of God. There was a stirring in the city and everyone was talking about what God was doing in our church. Amidst all this excitement, Sharon and I felt a void in our lives. We could not describe it then, but we knew there had to be more God could offer. We were thankful for every blessing, but we just could not be satisfied anymore. Our prayers changed. "Lord, we want more! We are tired of just playing church. We desperately want more of You!" We became so desperate that we wanted to quit the ministry if God did not use us in a greater way. Please understand that the Lord was really working in Bloemfontein. On the surface, things were great! But we felt like we'd reached the place in our lives where we just went through the motions of pastoring a church, keeping people satisfied, and earning our pay at the end of every month. In the natural, we had nothing to complain about. We were young, but the Lord was about to show us what He wanted for us and not what we had in mind. Just like Gideon, we tried to avoid the enemy and kept ourselves busy with the things of the ministry, in our own "winepress-reality."

✕ We entered into a time of frustration that kept us awake ✕ for many nights. On top of our frustration we started feeling guilty for being frustrated! Does that make sense? We looked at what God was doing, and yet, we wanted more.

God, the Unseen One, who sat under a tree close to us was about to show us more. He manifested Himself in a very real, tangible way that changed our lives forever! God started to change us with a Reality Check.

I'm With You

The Lord is with you, Gideon. What a wonderful message! This message would make the day for most Christians. Even though Gideon was not aware of the presence of the Lord in his life, God *was* there. That is the truth. This Angel was God Himself! In the Old Testament, God revealed Himself as the Angel of the Lord. He did not tell a white lie just to make Gideon feel better. No, He was telling the truth and the truth was a reality. God cannot lie! Nothing could chase God away. There is not a situation or enemy from

25

which God must flee. In the worst of circumstances, God is the One able to sit under a tree without any worries. He is God! David wrote, in Psalm 139:12, *"Even the darkness hides nothing from You, but the night shines as the day; the darkness and the light are both alike to You."* Your life may be darkened by worries, fears or circumstances, but you must remember that God does not need night-vision equipment to see. He sees in the darkness just as in the light.

In our time of frustration, the first thing God spoke into our hearts was, "I am with you!" In the same way, God is telling you right now, "I am with you." That is part of the Divine Reality. You are not alone. You do not have to hide from the enemy. God is with you. You do not have to succumb to any situation. Just look around and you will see an oak tree and God waiting for you there. Look for the oak! The place of rest and comfort. The place of shade out of the scorching sun.

A Mighty Man in God's Eyes

But there is even more! *The Lord is with you, you mighty man of [fearless] courage.* God is saying these encouraging uplifting words to a man; poor, wretched, hiding because of his fear of the enemy. Again, God did not lie to Gideon to make him feel better. God meant every word. How can this be?

God moves within the realms of His own Reality. He speaks from it, He leads from it, and He provides from it. He calls every believer to join Him in it. Everything He does is in relation to His Reality. Although we will never really understand Him or be able to figure Him out, there is a way to know Him. We need to rise up into the sphere of His Reality and live in it.

God speaks to Gideon out of the Divine Reality. God sees in him a mighty man of fearless courage. That is his destiny. God called him to be just that! Gideon is not that man yet because he is living in the reality of his situation. God is speaking prophetically into Gideon's life, calling those things that are not yet as if they are.

Unfulfilled Prophecy

Before we go any further, I would like to interject something about a prophetic word in our lives. Many of us have received a word from God at some point in our lives— prophesies of what God wants concerning our lives. Some have been fulfilled, but others remain dormant in our lives. Sometimes it seems as if the words of God for our lives will never be fulfilled. We tend to think we cannot do anything to make it happen, but there is something we can do. Remember, every word God speaks to us is spoken out of the sphere of God's Reality, just like with Gideon. If we are consumed by our situation and live in such a way that it is more real to us than the Divine Reality, we will never see eye-to-eye with the words of God in our lives. It will seem impossible for the prophesies to be fulfilled. We need to see, live, and function in the Divine Reality. Nothing is impossible with God, and the same applies to those living in this Godly sphere. The Bible says *We can do all things through Christ who strengthens me* (Philippians 4:13). We must connect to God's frequency, to understand His words and promises to us. Then we will never misinterpret any prophesy from God.

He Listened But Did Not Hear a Word

Gideon learned this the hard way. He did not even hear or recognize the prophecy. All he heard was: "The Lord is with you." He immediately analyzed these five words against the reality of his situation. The answer he came up with did not compute:

*O sir, if the Lord is with us, why is all this befallen us?
And where are all His wondrous works of which our
fathers told us.... But now the Lord has forsaken us
and given us into the hand of Midian (Judges 6:13).*

Let us look at his answer. I want to show you how deaf
and blind we can be, when caught up in our circumstances.
First of all he said: *"Oh sir,"* He did not recognize he was
actually speaking to the Lord Himself. He did not realize the
Maker of all things was standing in front of him. If he did, he
would definitely speak of much more important things. He
had the opportunity to ask the Lord all the questions he did
not understand concerning creation, the angels, God Himself,
but he ended up moaning and groaning about his situation.

Many times when God speaks to us today, we do
exactly the same thing. We either do not recognize His voice
when He speaks to us, or we start to moan and groan about
our situation, not giving Him much opportunity to speak
into our lives.

Secondly, Gideon did not listen to the words of the Lord
intently. God said: *"Gideon, I am with you."* Gideon
replied: *"If the Lord is with us...."* God did not speak about
others. He spoke about Him and Gideon.

God is interested in the individual. He is a personal God
who loves every person the same. He is not a respecter of
persons, but He has a special, different plan for each life. He
wants to communicate His plan for you personally, through
His Holy Spirit. When He speaks to you, remember He
speaks to you—not to someone else. I have been in many
meetings where someone had a "word from God for the
church," but actually it was a word from God for that individual. We must come to a point where we receive God's
Word and the prompting of His Spirit for ourselves. Even if
God gives you a word for someone else or the church as a

whole, remember you are a part of the church and the word is firstly for you and then for others. This is how I see every sermon the Lord gives me to preach. First, God is preaching it to me and I have to respond. After that, He allows me to preach it to others.

A third point I want to share with you is that Gideon's experience with God was based on the past and on what he had heard about the Lord. He is speaking about what God did with Israel in Egypt many generations before. Gideon was not in Egypt. He did not see the Hand of God moving through Moses and Joshua. He did not see the Nile turned to blood. He did not experience what it feels like to walk through the Red Sea on dry ground. He did not see the pillar of fire or eat the manna or drink from the fountain in the rock. He heard all about that, but he did not have any experience with God, himself. He believed in the wondrous works of God—to him, it was a historical truth—but they were not a reality.

God: Truth or Reality?

So many people today believe in the awesome power of God. They believe God is moving by His Spirit all over the earth. They hear of what He did in previous revivals, and they even get excited about it. But their experience of the power of God is nothing more than a knowledge of the stories of Jesus written in the Gospels. They read of men who were used of God to bring revival in the past, but it never dawns on them that God is still the same. He is still moving today. He is still pouring out His Spirit in the lives of people, changing them from glory unto glory, never to be the same again. Miracles happen in the lives of many people, everyday, as they experience the touch of the Master's Hand in their lives. It is available for every indi-

29

vidual irrespective of their name, color, ability, past, financial situation, or influence.

God is more than mere history. Hebrews 13:8 says: *Jesus Christ is [always] the same, yesterday, today, [yes] and forever (to the ages).* He is always the same. Circumstances do not determine how He is. He does not get out of bed on the wrong foot. In fact, He never sleeps. He does not have a bed! Today He is the same wonder-working, miracle-doing, delivering, forgiving, Awesome God as He ever was or ever will be. No enemy can take that away from Him and no problem you can have will be able to crush His reputation. If you let Him, He will come through for you as He did for millions over all the ages. He is not just the Truth, but He is also **Reality!**

One night, in a revival meeting in Kill Devil Hills, on the Outer Banks of North Carolina, the power of the Holy Spirit fell in the church during the praise and worship. In the Spirit, I saw a cloud of God's Glory entering the sanctuary. Sharon, still playing the piano, was hit by the power of God. She started to minister through prophetic song for more than an hour. The whole night was turned into a Night of Victory by the Holy Spirit. Some people were paralyzed in their seats by the power of God and others fell to the ground. Some stood in His presence, bathing in His glory, while others shouted for joy and victory. Everyone in the building became aware of the presence of God. They were caught up into the Reality of God. God was saying that victory could be found on a hill called Calvary! One lady, usually very shy in the natural, walked up the steps of the platform. She turned to the people, lifted her hands and shouted in a very loud voice: "Victory! I'm climbing the hill of Victory!" She overcame her shyness by entering into the realm of God's Reality. Needless to say, many miracles took place that night.

Even up to the writing of this book, people are still testifying about the impact of the Night of Victory in their lives. That night was recorded and the tape has been a blessing to us. Every time we listen to the tape we become aware of the Divine Reality all over again! Months after the meeting, that same lady is still testifying of her encounter with God.

Food for Thought:

- *Reality Check*: God is with you.
- *Reality Check*: You are what He says you are.
- *Reality Check*: Do not settle for anything less.

Not by Might Nor by Power

The Lord turned to him and said, "Go in this your might, and you shall save Israel from the hand of Midian. Have I not sent you?" (Judges 6:14).

"How did you get through your season of desperation?" I know you must have been pondering on this question for several pages. Well, now where was I? Oh yes...

Back in Bloemfontein, in the parsonage. In this time of desperation we prayed, pleaded and prayed even more, but it seemed as if heaven turned to brass! No answers, nothing. The hunger for God in us was like a slumbering volcano preparing for eruption. The pressure started to build in us to a point where it was unbearable. Nobody knew what we were going through. We did not tell anyone. To the regular church-going people, it was life as usual. Interestingly enough, we later found out that many people in the church were going through similar frustration!

I was becoming concerned for Sharon. Pressure tends to show its effects more clearly in women than in men. In women, pressure tends to "flow outward," showing itself quickly—while in men, it usually "flows inward," slumbering until an eruption takes place. It has potential to ruin lives in both instances. Sharon and I, for that matter, could not hide the pressure anymore. It became so intense that we took a two-month vacation to get away from the "pressures of the church." It was the two longest months of our lives. Little did we know what was about to happen.

"Lord, we give You two months to change our lives, otherwise we will quit the ministry and do something else. And Lord, that's a promise!" Desperate people pray dangerous prayers. We did not pray this prayer lightly. We were serious. We just could not go on like this.

As the days dragged by, something started to happen in our lives. The heavens opened slowly and we started to see the Unseen One who was always so close by. We went to a conference and each had an encounter with God that changed our lives. It was not the evangelist or the venue or the fellowship with others that changed us—it was because of our hunger for God. At the end of our desperation, our revival began! I will share more about this encounter in Chapter 8.

Friend, you may be going through similar circumstances. Not the same, because every person goes through unique things in their lives, but similar. The Lord wants victory for all of us. He wants all of us to live the higher life. He put in us all the potential to rise up and change our own generation.

The Bible says David served his own generation (Acts 13:36). Yes, *you* are called by God to be a life-changer. Don't be history; make it! God does not look at your ability. In fact, He does not need your ability. *With God nothing is ever impossible* (Luke 1:37). He does not need your strength. When you are weak He is strong (2 Corinthians 12:9b). He does not need your wisdom and ideas.

> *The foolish thing [that has its source in] God is wiser than men.... God selected what in the world is low-born and insignificant, and branded and treated with contempt, even the things that are nothing, that He might depose and bring to nothing the things that are, so that mortal man should boast in the presence of God* (1 Corinthians 1:25,28-29).

The Need for a New Miracle

Let's look at Gideon once again. He did not have a clear understanding of what the Lord told him. He thought it was all over. He thought it would take a miracle of the past to get him and the rest of Israel out of this mess. "If only God can do it again..." Does that sound familiar? He was wrong. He needed God to do something new, not an old miracle of the past! We need a present, fresh one for today. Tomorrow, we will once again need another. The other day, I read a striking poster in a Christian bookstore. It said:

> *When you live in the past with its mistakes and regrets, it is hard.*
>
> *I am not there. My Name is not I was.*
>
> *When you live in the future with its problems and fears, it is hard.*
>
> *I am not there. My Name is not I will be.*

*When you live in this moment, it is not hard. I am here.
My Name is I AM*

—*Helen Mallicoat*

Why have we become experts on the past and future
moves of God, but we know so little about what is needed
today?

> *Behold, I am doing a new thing!* **Now** *it springs forth;
> do you not perceive and know it and will you not give
> heed to it? I will even make a way in the wilderness
> and rivers in the desert* (Isaiah 43:19).

God knew how little Gideon had going for him. He
knew of the lack of power and the feelings of despair and
worthlessness, but He looked from His Divine Reality
into Gideon's life. The only thing Gideon needed to suc-
ceed in life was God's power. Nothing more and nothing
less. So many people settle for less and fail miserably.
Others try to add their own mixture of pride, greed, and
wisdom to God's power and they, too, amount to nothing. It is *not by might, not by power, but by My Spirit
says the Lord of hosts* (Zechariah. 4:6). Settle for the gen-
uine, authenticated, real power of God.

Power is Packed in His Calling

*"Gideon, if you let go and let God have His way, you will do
mighty exploits!"* Wherever God demonstrates and makes
His power available to individuals, it is always welded
together with a Divine calling. If you are looking for His
power, look only as far as His calling for your life! *"Have I
not sent you?"* Gideon could never answer the Divine call or
accomplish the victory on his own. The task was totally
beyond his reach. He needed help from God. Actually, all he
had to do was obey and God would do the rest.

This is a very important lesson to learn. God will always call you to do something that is beyond your reach in His Kingdom. You will never be able to say "I have done it on my own. I have reached Your destiny for me." You see, God takes the credit. It is Him doing the work through you. He produces results through His grace and through your faithfulness. Everything is God. That is the reason why John said these powerful words: *He must increase, but I must decrease. [He must grow more prominent; I must grow less so]* (John 3:30). Thomas Muthee, Senior Pastor of the Prayer Cave in Kiambu, Kenya, and a good friend, always says: "God will never give you a job equal to your resources!"

As the disciples looked up at the sky, waving as Jesus departed to heaven, they faced the biggest task anyone could dream of. The Lord entrusted them to spread His message through the whole earth. The words of Jesus still rang in their minds:

> *You shall receive power (ability, efficiency, and might) when the Holy Spirit has come upon you, and you shall be My witnesses in Jerusalem and all Judea and Samaria and to the ends (the very bounds) of the earth* (Acts 1:8).

It was not up to them to produce the results. All they had to do was receive the power. In Acts 2, we read of the wonderful way they received it. They did not simply receive the ability to speak in tongues; they did not merely hear the sound like a mighty rushing wind; they did not just see the tongues of fire on them; they were not only overcome with power so that many people thought they were drunk. They received the Holy Spirit Himself— the Third Person of the Holy Trinity. In Him is the power of

God! He is a real companion and friend. It was as if the same Jesus they walked with and talked with and ate with, the One Who just departed from them, was manifested inside of them! No longer would they have to search for Him and follow Him in the natural realm. They were to be guided into a new realm filled with adventure and excitement. Now every miracle and sermon was going to be born in them by the Holy Spirit. Through faithfulness and obedience, they would release the same power into the lives of everyone who listened to them.

The power of God can never be separated from the Person of the Holy Spirit. If you find His power, you find Him. If you find Him, you are given power! Are you looking for power? Look no further than the Holy Spirit. Many sought power in many ways, but those who found it in the Holy Spirit made a difference in this world. Their legacy lives on. Look at the disciples: Peter, James, John, and the others. Look at Paul, Timothy, and Titus. Read about their power, which came from their closeness to the Holy Spirit. Read about giants of faith like Smith Wigglesworth, John G. Lake, Finney, Wesley, and others. They found power when they found the Lord—and left so much behind for you and me because of that power.

That is the realm God wants you to live in! Do not look for Him in the realm of the natural. You will find Him in the Spirit. God is calling you to explore the realm of the supernatural with Him. Go on that expedition with Him. He wants to take you to places you have never been before and He wants to use you in greater ways than you thought possible. The sky is the limit. Soar to new heights in Him. Today, He is saying to you: "Have I not called you?" How far are you prepared to go with Him? How hungry for Him are you? How desperate have you become? Remember, at the end of your desperation, revival is waiting! The end of your way that now seems to go nowhere is just the beginning of great things in the Spirit. It is the gateway to the realm of God's Reality. Will you enter through it?

Food for Thought:

- A new miracle is what you need.
- Supernatural power is available for supernatural deeds.
- The realm of the natural grows dim next to the Divine Reality.

A Lesson in Humility

Gideon said to Him, "Oh Lord, how can I deliver Israel? Behold, my clan is the poorest in Manasseh, and I am the least in my father's house." The Lord said to him, "Surely I will be with you, and you shall smite the Midianites as one man" (Judges 6:15-16).

God chooses an unlikely candidate to perform a very huge and important task. Looking in the natural, we would not have chosen Gideon. He just did not have the right credentials. His family was poor and lowly. He had nothing going for him. Even in his father's house there was more important and better material. Gideon was not only a member of the poorest and smallest family in Manasseh, he was the poorest and smallest member in that family! To top it all, he was fearful for his own life, hiding from the enemy. Definitely not material heroes are made of.

Still God chose this poor, small wretch of a man to be a hero. You see, God makes His decisions based not on the natural realm, on appearance and natural fact—He makes it based on the Divine Reality. He knows once Gideon is elevated into His realm, he would become that mighty man of fearless courage. He would be the hero stories are made of!

Gideon was all but puffed up about his life, not even given the fact and reality of this visitation from God Himself. If anyone could be excited about this news, it would be Gideon. Wasn't he the one to whom God Almighty appeared? Out of thousands of other young men, he was the one, the Main Man. Here he was, talking to God personally—in Old Testament times, that says quite a lot! He could easily have adapted an attitude of "I'm the man!"

Such a boastful, big-headed attitude has been the downfall of many in the past and will be in the future. God hates pride. Someone once said: "Nobody is Somebody in the Kingdom of God." Everyone who wants to be used of Him must be humble. In the realm of the natural, we are nothing. It is when we get plugged into God and raised to His realm and function in the Divine Reality, that we are transformed into mighty men and women of God—people who can do exploits.

Just look at Jesus, the Son of the Living God. He is the Prince of heaven. Everything exists because of Him. He made time, light, planets, stars, ants, you, and me. He is the Center. Everything revolves around Him. Yet He came to the earth as a helpless baby, became the son of a carpenter, lived in Nazareth and not in a royal palace in Jerusalem. Someone once said: "He was man enough to drink the milk in Mary's breast, yet God enough to have made that milk!" He loved, healed, and shared. He served! The Prince of heaven came to serve mankind. Wow! That would have been so difficult for someone who struggled with pride. Not for Jesus, though. He showed us true humility. He did not have to say, "Hey, look how humble I am." He just was. Pride will always try to advertise what looks like humility. Humility will expose a servant's heart.

You may think you are an unlikely candidate for God. The fact is: God specializes in "liking the unlikely" and using them mightily. You may think you are poor without any means to do anything. The fact is: God does not need your financial support to accomplish something. You need His! You may think you do not belong to an important and influential family and will not one day become someone special, based on your family name. The fact is: when you invited Jesus into your heart, you were born into the biggest, richest, noblest, and most influential family around. You are not just a mere distant relative, but a son or daughter of the Most High God Himself! Now you are a fellow prince or princess of heaven! The moment you are hit with this realization, it will not give you a big head—instead, it will give you a big heart.

The Jellyfish Attitude

Have you ever walked on the beach and come across a jellyfish? It is somewhat transparent and has tentacles underneath it. In the water, it drifts along with the currents and although it has a limited means to propel itself through the water, it mostly relies on the current to take it where it needs to go. Some jellyfish will sting you when you touch them. This is a built-in defense mechanism. A jellyfish has no eyes, no vision. It floats around in darkness, simply existing.

43

Many Christians have this same attitude. I call it the Jellyfish Attitude. They have no backbone and feel insecure and transparent, almost naked in the midst of people. They have a total misconception of what biblical humility really is. They get trampled upon by anyone and everyone, all in the name of being a true, humble Christian. In the eyes of the world, they are wimps who cannot do anything for themselves. They function best by just "riding" the tides of their circumstances. They have been lied to by the enemy, who will take something holy, like Biblical humility, and distort it into a unholy giving-into-backbonelessness. This is false humility. The self-protective sting of a hands-off mentality will be felt by anyone who comes along and reaches out to such Christians. These people find it hard to trust others and doubt every good motive. They live isolated by a self-built wall surrounding them to keep them from being hurt again. Worst of all, they have no vision. They live in spiritual blindness, trying to exist through another day.

This is where the enemy kept Gideon. This was the source of his fear and defeat. He looked at himself in the realm of the natural and saw nothing but a worm. He thought he was humble, but in fact he was robbed. The enemy stole his backbone! He was nothing but intimidated. Propelled by fear, he isolated himself in the winepress.

True Humility

Biblical humility revolves around the awe you have for God in your life. It is a constant realization that Jesus in you, is greater and bigger than anything in your life, even you! It is the fruit that grows on you every time you enter into the realm of the Divine Reality, where everything else grows dim in the Light of His Glory and Grace. True humility is to let God be God in your life because you know without Him you are nothing. It is the submission of everything to Him so you can be used in His purposes, touching the lives of others with the Glory of God. In short, it is complete dependency upon Him in everything!

Do not let the enemy distort your mind into believing his version of what humility really is. If you want to learn about humbleness, look at the life of "Mr. Humble," Himself: Jesus Christ. Never did He give an inch to the enemy. He did not go with the flow when the flow was going in the wrong direction. He did not right any wrongs even when the wrongs seemed right. He stood for who He was and even more: He stood for His Father who sent Him to this earth. He did not give in to the pressures of the natural, fleshly realm. He surrendered to the prompting of the Holy Spirit in the Divine Reality. He is the Son of God, our Savior, Friend, and Example. You are not Him—but you are called to become like Him. You are the glove and He is the Hand in that glove. Once the glove is on the hand, it can function in complete unity with the hand, doing everything the hand does. The glove has the same potential as the hand—with one difference: the hand can function without the glove, but the glove, without the hand in it, is no more than a mere piece of cloth or leather.

Be just like Him. Nothing more—and surely nothing less.

Gideon had to understand the concept of true humbleness. God said to him: *I will be with you and you will smite the Midianites as one man.*

When God is with you, you can smite any enemy. It is not you. The difference is God. As long as you are the glove on His Hand, no enemy can wear you on his hand.

As Gideon focused on the natural, he saw his father, Joash, and the fact that he (Gideon) was the least in his father's house. God wanted him to know the Divine Reality.

Gideon had a new house and a new Father. He was a citizen of heaven living in the secret place of the Most High.

In the Divine Reality, you are part of a new family—the family of God. You have a new clan called the champions. You have access to a new territory, the secret place of the Most High. *He who dwells in the secret place of the Most High shall abide under the shadow of the Almighty* (Psalm 91:1, NKJV). *Therefore if any person is [ingrafted] in Christ (the Messiah) he is a new creation (a new creature altogether); the old [previous moral and spiritual condition] has passed away. Behold, the fresh and new has come!* (2 Corinthians 5:17).

Food for Thought:

- To be big, you must become small.
- Humility always has a backbone!
- You are the glove and God is the Hand in you.

The Presence of the Lord

*T*he Lord said to him, "Surely I will be with you..." (Judges 6:16).

If there is one thing every Christian needs extra Divine revelation into, it is in the area of God's Presence in their lives. We read in Isaiah 55: *Seek the Lord while He may be found.* There is coming a day that the Lord will not be found by those who seek Him. It will be too late! That day will be a terrible day for all living creatures: being cut off from the Presence of the Lord. As tragic as it may seem, what is almost just as bad is the many people living their lives now in complete defiance of the Presence of the Lord. They are ignorant of it! I am not just speaking about worldly people, but many Christians, as well. There are Christians who can go through a whole day working hard, being occupied and minding their own business, without giving one thought to God and heaven's business. Without offering one prayer, even so simple as, "Hello, Father, I love you." or "Thank you, God, for today's oxygen!" Just business as usual. Yet God is with you all the way, everyday!

No Hacking Needed!

Today, if you seek the Lord you will find Him. He is available to you. You can tap into His awesome and powerful Presence without having to "hack" your way through various security measures. You simply have to seek the Lord! If only you knew what is available to you. Stop seeking answers in astrology, living according to some message hidden in a star somewhere in our galaxy, when you can talk to the One Who planned and laid out the entire universe! Stop running after technology, wondering with awe what they'll come up with next. Rather, run after the One Who does not need a computer chip to figure out how to keep the planets in place! You do not need a degree to access God's presence. You do not even have to work hard to get to it. You can, and should, live and move and have your being **in** Him. Let us take a closer look at the three dimensions of the Presence of the Lord.

His Omnipresence

God is everywhere all the time. There are no secrets that can be kept from Him. He knows exactly what is going on where, when, and how—who is involved and what caused it to happen. David writes, in Psalm 139, that there is no place he can go on the face of the earth to hide from the presence of God.

Where can I go from Your Spirit? Or where can I flee from Your presence? If I ascend into heaven, You are there; If I make my bed in hell (Sheol), behold, You are there. If I take the wings of the morning, and dwell in the uttermost parts of the sea, even there Your hand shall lead me, and Your right hand shall hold me. If I say, "Surely the darkness shall fall on me," even the night shall be light about me; indeed, the darkness shall not hide from You, but the night shines as the day; the darkness and the light are both alike to You (Psalm 139:7-12, NKJV).

This manifestation of the presence of God is a security to the Believer! There is no place you can go or be taken to where you will be on your own! They locked the prison door behind Paul and Silas and thought it would teach them a lesson—only to find, the next morning, an open cell filled with the Glory of the Lord and a prison filled with believers! God visited them in prison during the night. Gideon was hiding from the enemy in the winepress and the Lord was close to him, sitting under the oak as the Unseen One.

You could be shipwrecked on a desert island and still you will not be alone. You can drive to work in your car and know the Creator of heaven and earth is with you. You could be stuck in traffic on Interstate 95, just outside Washington DC, and sense the presence of God rather than the agitation of neighboring drivers. You can be traveling to Africa, China, or even Mars. You could even be lost without a map, but you'll not be without the presence of God. Jesus told His disciples, *I am with you all the days to the [very] close and consummation of the age* (Matthew 28:20). What a security! What a wonder! This fact should satisfy every fearful Christian's heart. When the first missionaries reached the Bushmen of the Kalahari Desert in Southern Africa, they were amazed at these primitive, loving people who had no problem accepting there is a God in heaven. They always believed someone great was responsible for all the goodness the land had to offer, every drop of precious rain or dew. When told Jesus died on the cross for man's sin, they wanted to know what sin was. There was no word in their vocabulary for sin. The missionaries tried to explain. "It is all bad things like fighting with the people that you come across." They wanted to know why one would want to fight with people you love anyway! They are such loving, forgiving people. These Bushmen, totally isolated from Christianity or any other religion, lived their lives according to a very high moral and social standard! I believe it is because of the Omnipresence of God. The Omnipresence of God may or may not do much for the Unbeliever—to the Believer, however, it is an anchor to hold on to; a reality that cements you to your Creator.

His Indwelling Presence

The Lord's Indwelling Presence in the life of the Believer is the second manifestation of His Presence. This is the Christian's lifeline. It is through the Indwelling Presence that we are changed, everyday, into His likeness. Through the Indwelling Presence of God in your life, your character is formed and molded. The Fruit of the Spirit is cultivated and grows by and through the Indwelling Presence of the Lord. *I am the Vine: you are the branches. Whoever lives in Me and I in him bears much (abundant) fruit* (John 15:5).

God's Indwelling Presence in our lives is the 24-hour hotline connecting earth and heaven. It is God's info-line which gives us unlimited access to the realm of God (the Divine Reality) and it is free of charge!

Have you ever wondered what God meant when He said in His Word that we needed to *"Pray without ceasing?"* If we were to interpret this Scripture in the realm of the natural, we would have to be in our prayer closets twenty-four hours a day! That is not what God meant. How would we be able to *"Go into all the world"* and proclaim the Gospel? To pray without ceasing simply means to be connected to God through His Indwelling Presence! He in you and you in Him.

This is the most important manifestation of the presence of the Lord in our lives. On this level we are truly changed to be more like Jesus. Through His Indwelling Presence the fruit of the Holy Spirit grows in us. The Indwelling Presence of the Lord in our lives gives credibility to our testimonies and makes other people want to have what we've got. Psalm 1:1-3 (NKJV) speaks of someone having the Indwelling Presence of the Lord in their lives:

> *Blessed is the man who walks not in the counsel of the ungodly, nor stands in the path of sinners, nor sits in the seat of the scornful; but his delight is in the law of the Lord, and in His law he meditates day and night. He shall be like a tree planted by the rivers of water, that brings forth its fruit in its season, whose leaf also shall not whither; and whatever he does shall prosper.*

The Omnipresence and Indwelling Presence of the Lord both operate through the faith of the believer. Many days he will feel alone, not sensing God's presence, but that does not mean that God is on a leave of absence for that moment. Through faith, we know God is nearer to us than the nose on our face! Our feeling or lack thereof does not make God appear or disappear in our lives.

51

His Manifest Presence

The third manifestation of the Presence of the Lord is His Manifest Presence. This is where the Lord openly and tangibly manifests Himself or His power in your life. In many meetings when we sing and worship the Lord, suddenly you can sense and feel God's Presence in the place. You become aware of Him in all His Glory and you are even filled with fear and reverence. You stand in awe of His majesty and all human influence and charisma melts away before His Splendor. The stage is set for miracles, signs, and wonders to take place. The Unseen God has manifested His presence in a real and tangible way.

The Manifest Presence always comes with a purpose. God does not need to show off with His power. He is God! Jesus performed miracles only when someone needed one! He was the Son of God, whether people believed it or not! He fed 5,000 people because they were hungry. He changed water into wine to rescue a red-in-the-face host from extreme humiliation. He walked on the water to save the disciples from a sinking ship. He healed so many because they were sick! He always responded to the needs of people. When He manifests His Presence, something always happens. Healing, miracles, manifestations, deliverance, gifts of the Spirit, etc. People will be touched, blessed, and changed in the Manifest Presence of God. It is what I call the believer's jump-start. It will bring you to a spiritual high. You receive healing through the Manifest Presence and you maintain your healing through the Indwelling Presence.

The Manifest Presence is temporary in nature. After a while, this presence will lift from you. The feeling or tangible Presence will make way to the Indwelling Presence through faith. Some Christians make the mistake of trying to live in and maintain the Manifest Presence. They want to **feel** God's presence all the time. The problem is that your feelings can easily mislead you. One day you will **feel** close to God and another day you will **feel** removed from Him. God wants us to believe in Him and exercise our faith concerning His presence in our lives.

The Manifest Presence comes suddenly and sometimes unexpectedly; not just in meetings, but where and when the Lord wants to touch people through you or change an area of your life. Many times in our own lives, the Manifest Presence of the Lord comes over us in stores, malls, and public places. When that happens, Sharon and I know there is ministry to be done. Someone needs God in a special way. God desires to touch someone through us. The Manifest Presence is geared toward ministry. When the anointing comes upon you, so strong that you can sense or feel it, it is God's way to let you know it is time to minister to someone. This does not mean that you cannot minister without feeling the anointing or sensing the Manifest Presence. Do not count too much on your feelings. The most powerful miracles in our ministry came when God's Manifest Presence flowed through us without us feeling it! My personal experience is that the more I cultivate and yield to the Indwelling Presence of the Lord, the stronger and more frequently I am visited by His Manifest Presence.

Let us look at the life of Gideon again. The first time we find God in Gideon's life is where God is the Unseen One sitting under the tree near Gideon. This represents God's Omnipresence. Gideon did not know or feel like God was with him, but God was! The fact that Gideon was oblivious to God's presence does not mean that God was not there. It is said that an ostrich will sometimes, in the face of danger or a difficult situation, bury his head in the ground. He will then hope or imagine the danger or situation is not there because he cannot see it! Many people think, when they cannot see or feel the Lord, that He is not interested in being a part of their lives anymore. I call this the Ostrich Attitude. We laugh when we read this, but too many of us—just like Gideon—pull the same stunt in real life!

At a given point in time, God manifested His presence in Gideon's life. God, the Unseen One, became God—up close and personal. For Gideon, all the wondering of where God was all this time was over. Now he knew beyond any doubt that the Lord was with him. He was speaking to Him and God was answering him in a real and wonderful way. This encounter in the Manifest Presence of God changed Gideon's life and set him on a Divine course to become the hero God wanted him to be.

God revealed the road Gideon had to take to become this hero, through His Indwelling Presence. Even during the powerful encounter with the Manifest Presence of God, Gideon had many questions. He did not understand everything. God answered him by merely saying: "I will be with you." In other words, "You will need My Indwelling Presence to guide you along the way." Things become clear in God's Indwelling Presence. Now I know this happened in the Old Covenant, when the Holy Spirit was not yet sent to live in people. I know many of you are thinking that the Lord moved *upon* people in the Old Testament rather than *in* them. I am merely making a point: if God was with a person like Gideon, who lived in terms of the Old Covenant, how much more we, who live in terms of the New Covenant and are filled with the Spirit of the Lord, should experience the Presence of the Lord in our lives!

Take a few moments and look into your life and situation. Identify these three dimensions of God's presence in your life. Know that He is there (everywhere) with you. Also, think of the times He manifested His presence in your life. Maybe it was in a powerful meeting or during a time of prayer in your prayer closet. Can you remember the awe and tremendous power involved? How that encounter changed your life? Now focus on the Indwelling Presence. Are you sensitive and open toward that lifeline? Are you plugged into heaven or have you lost your connection? People who have identified and understood these different dimensions of God's presence have excelled in ministry and were mightily used by God in ways they themselves could never imagine.

Food for Thought:

- God's Omnipresence is your Security.
- God's Indwelling Presence is your Lifeline.
- God's Manifest Presence is your Jump-start.

A Sign from Heaven

Gideon said to Him, "If now I have found favor in your sight, then show me a sign that it is You Who talks with me" (Judges 6:17).

On your way home after a wonderful meeting where you felt the anointing flowing through you and God speaking to you, you find yourself praying aloud, "Lord, if this anointing is really from You, give me a sign: let all the traffic lights from the church to my house be green!" I know many friends, including myself, who have prayed a similar prayer before you, so don't worry... you are not alone.

It is natural for people to look for signs. Someone once said that everything bad happens in threes. People started believing this and every time they found themselves in a bad situation they saw it as a sign, counting how many mishaps were to follow to change their luck. A life guided by such superstitious thought becomes very complicated. The Bible gives us a much better and more simplistic approach to life. In this chapter, we are going to take a look at the role of signs in the life of a believer.

There are three main types of signs:

1. Signs of Faith (to believe in God).
2. Signs of Confirmation.
3. Signs and Wonders as Manifestations of the Holy Spirit.

Let us look at the first type.

1. Signs of Faith

These are signs people seek in order to believe in God, His Word, or Messengers. The Pharisees could not see that Jesus was the Messiah. They did not believe in Him because they did not want to. One day, a great crowd followed Jesus.

> *And a great multitude came to Him, bringing with them the lame, the maimed, the blind, the dumb, and many others, and they put them down at His feet; and He cured them. So that the crowd was amazed when they saw the dumb speaking, the maimed whole, the lame walking, and the blind seeing; and they recognized and praised and thanked and glorified the God of Israel* (Matthew 15:30-39).

The signs, in this case miracles, made them believe in Jesus. The signs made them stay with Jesus for three whole days, even without food. Signs from God will have that effect on you. They speak to your heart. Their message is clear and loud. Their words are piercing and bold. They remove doubt and fear and weld awe, love, and faith on the metal of the soul.

Jesus was not finished yet. He already healed the sick, but now He was about to feed the multitudes. Until now only a few people experienced the signs (miracles) first-hand while many looked on. Only those whom He healed could really tell of the awesome miracle the Lord gave them. Now the Lord wanted everyone not just to see, but to taste and see! He took seven loaves and a few small fish, and multiplied them to feed a crowd made up of 4,000 men plus the women and children! Seven baskets of food were left over— another sign for the people to behold.

In the very next verse, we read about two other groups of people, the Pharisees and Sadducees. They *came up to Jesus, and they asked Him to show them a sign (spectacular miracle) from heaven [attesting His divine authority]* (Matthew 16:1). Where were they all this time? In the last few days alone Jesus had healed the sick and fed thousands of people with seven loaves and a few small fish. Were these signs not spectacular enough? Were they not the kind of signs from heaven these religious men were looking for? How blind can you get?

The Pharisees did see all the signs Jesus performed. They were present as the splendor of the Messiah shone through His actions, but they were unmoved. Jesus said to them that they would be given no sign except for the sign of Jonah. Just as Jonah spent three days in the belly of the fish, was rescued and preached salvation to Nineveh, Jesus would soon spend three days in the belly of death and be resurrected to bring salvation to the world. **For the believer, this is the only sign to secure his or her faith.**

Paul writes, in 1 Corinthians 14:22, *Thus [unknown] tongues are meant for a [supernatural] sign, not for believers but for unbelievers [on the point of believing]*. Christians do not need signs in order to believe in God. Signs in the church attract unbelievers to God. I call them Signs of Faith.

A man in our church in Bloemfontein, South Africa, came to me one day saying, "Pastor, there are many visitors in our church on Sundays. Many of them are unbelievers. Can you please make sure that nothing too 'wild' will happen, like someone speaking in tongues? It might scare the visitors away." Knowing he meant well, I told him that the reason these folks were coming to the meetings in the first place was to see supernatural signs take place during the meetings. I have found many times it is believers who feel offended in meetings where the Glory of God is manifested in a mighty way—not the unbelievers, who are usually fascinated more than offended. Yes, they feel uncomfortable, but their discomfort is more a result of the conviction of the Holy Spirit working in their hearts, than the miraculous signs. Signs are **meant** for unbelievers!

2. Signs of Confirmation

These are signs believers seek as confirming something the Lord is doing in or through them. By themselves, these signs are futile and serve no purpose. Combine them with a Word from God and they come alive, burning in the spirit of the believer so powerfully that all else fades in the Reality of the Word God gave him or her.

Sometimes we hear the voice of God as a whisper, soft and gentle, as it resounds in our spirit. We can then ask the Lord to "amplify" the sound of His voice through a sign. Sometimes we hear God's voice amidst a cluttering of many voices inside us. Again we can ask the Lord to "amplify" His voice and distort all other voices in our ears by giving us a sign as confirmation. This is what Gideon was asking when he asked for a sign. He knew this was the most defining moment in his life. He knew God was doing great things in his life and the days of hiding in the winepress were over. He knew he would walk out of the hiding place facing the same enemy, the same circumstances, with the same abilities as before, but this time with a Word of promise from God. If he was to rise to the occasion, acting upon that Word, he had to rid himself of all doubt right away. How did he do it? He asked for a sign!

The devil can easily bring doubt to a Word you receive from the Lord. He knows math. He is very cunning in addition and subtraction. He'll add something to the Promise the Lord gave you in your heart or he'll blind you to a condition that will activate that Promise. A sign from God stops him in his tracks! It brings your focus back to what you should do; to the very thing the Lord placed at hand in your life.

This is one of the purposes of the Prophetic gift in the New Testament Church. Modern-day prophecies are not meant to serve as a Christian crystal ball that gives you insight into the future. Yes, there is a futuristic element in prophecy today—but it always agrees with God's Word in your heart concerning your life. New Testament prophecy has many facets. It brings correction as well as comfort. Prophecy sometimes is the God-given "sign" for many to confirm a direction God wants them to take in their life. *By the mouth of two or three witnesses every word shall be established* (2 Corinthians 13:1b, NKJV). As a believer, you are entitled to Divine confirmation.

On this note I must give a caution. I have come across some Christians constantly "looking" for confirmation. They will hunt for a prophetic word until they have ten or twelve. It seems that all they do is to gather promises and words. I want to point out that biblical confirmation means two or at most three signs (i.e. words, prophetic promises, etc.). After that, God wants us to act upon what we hear! God's purpose, with the promises He gives us, is not to stay unfulfilled until we get to heaven. After Gideon received the sign of confirmation, he acted! Signs of confirmation will thrust believers into action according to the Will and Direction of God for them, bringing fulfillment to prophetic promises.

I have heard of many people who received prophetic words from God—promises they held onto for dear life. They lived by them and knew their content by heart. They waited for the fulfillment—and died, waiting! Too many promises God gives stay unfulfilled. People even turn on God and blame Him for not doing what He promised! God is no liar! He is always ready to work supernaturally with His Word to fulfill it. In Mark 16:20, we read:

> *And they went out and preached everywhere, while the Lord kept working with them and confirming the message by the attesting signs and miracles that closely accompanied [it].*

Isaiah 55:11 says:

> *So shall My word be that goes forth out of My mouth: it shall not return to Me void [without producing any effect, useless], but it shall accomplish that which I please and purpose, and it shall prosper in the thing for which I sent it.*

We must align our lives in the very direction of the promises of God, without taking things into our own hands. Someone once said, "God does not need our help; He needs our cooperation."

Gideon's sign of confirmation came in the form of fire from a rock that burned up a sacrifice of meat and unleavened bread. Gideon prepared a sacrifice for God. He paid a price. It took time to prepare this meal. Remember, he was a poor man, hiding what precious wheat he had so the Midianites would not get to it. He had lost so much by the hand of the Midianites, that to prepare such a meal meant much to him. He felt it in his pocket. The Word and promises he received from the Lord were very important to him and he showed the Lord how important and precious they were. God always honors sacrifice! He wants to see what we do with the blessings and the promises He gives us. He honored Gideon's sacrifice by sending fire. Fire is a symbol of the Holy Spirit. If you want the fire of the Holy Spirit burning in your heart, you must make sacrifices. Show the Lord how important He is to you. Show Him how valuable His promises and Words are to you. He will always answer by giving you a sign of confirmation by the Holy Spirit. Will you pay the price?

3. Signs and Wonders as Manifestations of the Holy Spirit

There is in the Church today a fresh wave of manifestations, as the Holy Spirit brings refreshment and revival. Some people fall down under the power of the Holy Spirit when prayed for (Revelation 1:17). Others are filled with joy and excitement (Psalm 126; Romans 14:17). Some get drunk on the new wine of the Holy Spirit. They are so filled with the Holy Spirit that people ask the same question they asked Peter and the other disciples on the day of Pentecost: "What have you been drinking? Are you drunk?" Peter replied, *These are not drunk as you suppose, as it is only the third hour (nine in the morning). They are just filled with the Holy Ghost*" (Acts 2:15—in my own words). There are many other manifestations: shaking (Hebrews 12:26–28), trembling (1 Corinthians 2:3), dancing (Psalm

149:3), trances (Acts 10:10), boldness (Acts 4:13,29–31), weeping (Luke 6:21), and more.

People often ask if these manifestations are, in fact, from God—and, if so, what purpose do they have? We can dedicate a whole book to answering this question, but let me say this with regard to manifestations as signs from heaven: God will never contradict Himself. He will never say something in His Word and then do something that is totally opposite or different to His Word. He is the Truth so He can never lie to you, or in any way deceive you! Isn't that good news? Every manifestation must fit the criteria we find in God's Word. If someone in the Bible fell down because of the awesome power of the Lord in his or her life, then we know something similar might happen today. If someone trembled when God visited them in Bible times, we are bound to see a similar reaction to God's Glory today. If people were filled with joy when the Lord touched them in the Bible, then joy will be a part of our experience with God today. *Jesus Christ (the Messiah) is [always] the same, yesterday, today, [yes] and forever (to the ages)* (Hebrews 13:8). We can apply this principle to all manifestations.

Whenever the Holy Spirit moves in a meeting on a person's life and there is some kind of manifestation, it means this: God is working within that person's heart, bringing forth change. In the days and weeks to come, fruit will appear that will testify of the great and awesome work the Lord has done in that person's life. The fruit will always point to Jesus. He will always be glorified! This is very important. The work of the Holy Spirit is to glorify Jesus. Whether He blows like a wind in a meeting or flows like a river in a conference; whether He chooses to activate one or more of the nine gifts of the Holy Spirit in your life or manifest Himself in you through signs and wonders, He will always glorify Jesus Christ (John 16:14). He testifies of Jesus and brings you closer to Jesus. Always! Jesus Himself told the disciples that the Holy Spirit is *the Spirit of Truth Who comes (proceeds) from the Father. He [Himself] will testify regarding Me* (John 15:26). *But when He, the Spirit of Truth (the Truth-giving Spirit) comes, He will guide you into all the truth (the whole, full truth)* (John 16:13). Jesus said, in John 14:6: *I am the Way and the Truth and the Life; no one comes to the Father except by (through) Me.* Jesus Himself is the Truth the Holy Spirit will lead us in!

Someone once told me, while pastoring in South Africa, that we (our church) placed too much emphasis on the Holy Spirit. He called us "Holy Ghost fanatics" and felt nothing good could come of it. He accused us of being unbalanced. I knew his words were formed in a very hurting and lonely heart, but I went to the Lord with these accusations. I wanted to know how the Lord felt about them. I did not want to listen to someone I hardly knew and miss God in the process. I also did not want to be blinded by my own view, leading many astray because of pride lurking in my heart. The Lord spoke to me very clearly. He said: "Son, you cannot place too much emphasis on My Spirit. He is the Spirit of Truth and will always lead you to My Son, Jesus. If you continue to follow the Holy Spirit, you will end up in the arms of the Savior Himself!" My heart jumped inside me. When you follow the Holy Spirit, you are not placing Jesus second. You are actually getting closer to Him! There is no competition in the Godhead, seeing Who is more important. No, in heaven there is complete unity and cooperation. All disharmony was taken care of when God threw Satan out. In the Trinity, we have a God Who is **Three in One**. It is a mystery and we will never completely know all there is to know about God. Throughout history, people focused more on the Three of God, studying the Father, Son, and Holy Spirit, apart from each other, as you would study three different people. On the other hand, there were some who focused more on the One of God, melting them into One Person expressed in Three ways. My feeling is that we should focus on both aspects with equal vigor in our pursuit of more of God in our lives.

In closing, I just want to say this: I set my heart not on looking for signs from heaven like the Pharisees, but rather to seek an encounter with God. A touch from God personally in my life is what I need and want. A specific moment when God steps into my life and becomes an all-consuming Reality, so real and so strong that I am unable to ignore Him, unable to rationally pass Him off, unable to question my experience, unable to stay the same old person I was.

Food for Thought:

- Your faith in God will take you further than a sign from heaven.

- A sign from heaven will activate your faith in God.

- The power of God can be experienced.

Touched by God

Then the Angel of the Lord reached out the tip of the staff that was in His hand, and touched the meat and the unleavened cakes, and there flared up fire from the rock and consumed the meat and the unleavened cakes. Then the Angel of the Lord vanished from his sight (Judges 6:21).

Gideon was in the middle of an encounter with God and he did not even know it. His life was being touched—never to be the same again. To him, at this point, it was wonderful yet doubtful. He wanted to believe, but did not know if it really could be true. He asked for a sign, made his sacrifice, and now the moment of truth was at hand. The Lord was about to guarantee every word and promise with a touch from heaven. He was about to seal His words with fire. God wanted to activate the process of fulfillment supernaturally.

Throughout the Bible, we read of great men and women, mightily moved by the Lord, doing exploits in the kingdom of God. All had an encounter with the Living God. A specific moment where supernatural meets natural; where heaven touches earth; where Spirit meets flesh. A moment similar to what Gideon was experiencing, yet unique to every person.

Many would say the days of such encounters with God belong to Bible times, because God does not work that way anymore. I have often asked myself who these people think they are, to tell us what God can do today and how He does what He does today. Where did they get their information? Are they looking at their own experiences and do they write their theology based on them? This "if it did not happen to me, it cannot happen at all" attitude is rather common today. The mere lack of something we read of in the Bible today is not proof that God changed His method of operation. All that it proves to me is that I must conform my life to the Word, so the things that happened in God's Word may also happen in my life!

God touched Gideon's life through the sacrifice Gideon made. That was the point of contact—the point of entry to the Divine Reality. Let me tell you right now: God is quite willing to touch your life in such a real and special way that, when you read in the Bible of people who encountered God in miraculous ways, you will know exactly what they experienced! Let me share with you what happened to my wife, Sharon, and I, during such an encounter:

At this point I want to pick up from Chapter 4, where we were in Bloemfontein, South Africa. The void in our hearts was growing deeper day by day. At first we were able to ignore it and focus on the church and the work of the Lord, but in time it got to a point where all we could focus on was this emptiness inside us. We started crying out to the Lord. The more we cried out to Him, the more evident our need became. Our yearning exposed our need.

Every prayer we prayed started with, "Lord, we know there must be more." This went on for several months. One day we heard of a revival in Lakeland, Florida. We heard how the Lord poured out His Spirit and how many people were touched and changed by the power of the Lord. We knew we needed a touch from heaven, but we could not afford to go to that revival. The Lord spoke to me one day and asked: "Son, are you prepared to pay the price?" I realized that I was willing to take out a loan at the bank to buy a car, but was not prepared to do at least the same when it came to my spiritual benefit. Immediately, I said: "Lord, we will go to these meetings even if we have to go to the bank for help." This was a big sacrifice for us, but we determined in our hearts to go through with it. Within two weeks after we made this determination, God miraculously supplied every penny for the trip, including spending money. We joined with seven other pastors in our area and embarked on the trip of our lives.

We arrived early for the first meeting and wanted to register before the meeting. When Sharon and I walked into the building, we sensed the presence of the Lord in an incredible way. We both started crying. We did not even register, but instead went into the auditorium, found a seat and sobbed for an hour until the meeting started. This had never happened to us before. I turned to Sharon and said, "Can you feel it?" She nodded her head and cried even more.

After a while she asked me, "Darling, do you feel it?" and I winked at her and cried on. This continued through the praise and worship, the offering, and even into the sermon. Then the evangelist stopped preaching and walked in our direction. He called a brother right in front of us out and prayed for him. Then he called us out. We could not get up out of our seats! The presence of the Lord was heavy on us. At first we thought it was jet lag! (The flight from South Africa was over 17 hours!) The ushers helped us to the altar area.

The next thing I remember is laying on my back, on the floor, in front of 8,000 people! I knew the evangelist did not even touch me—yet, the power of the Lord knocked me off my feet! The same happened to Sharon: I looked at her, next to me, and saw she was "gone." It looked as if she was in a deep sleep. She later told me she had been with the Lord. She "woke" up two hours later.

It was not so with me. From the moment my body touched the carpet, I wanted to get up and get back to my pew. I tried to get up, but I could not. It felt as if my jacket was pinned to the floor. I was embarrassed and thought everyone was looking at me. I thought of my seven colleagues. What were they thinking? What were they going to say? After all, I had a reputation to protect. With much effort, I got on my hands and knees. I looked up and saw a pew about ten yards from me. I crawled to it because I could not walk. I dragged myself onto the pew and held on for life. I was disoriented. There was something wrong with my balance, I thought. I opened my eyes and saw I was sitting on the altar pews facing all the people! Nobody really paid any attention to me, but I felt like the whole world was looking at me. One of my friends, who was one of the pastors from our area, came down to me to help me sit up straight. He saw I was having a hard time sitting on this seat. When he touched me, the power of the Lord hit him and he was out on the floor for more than two hours!

The anointing on me started to lift after about an hour. If you think this is powerful, friend, you have not heard anything yet. I am unable to put into words what happened inside my spirit during this time. The external is easy to describe, but how do you describe with earthly words a heavenly experience?

Throughout that week we attended the meetings. There was not a second that Sharon or I spent unaware of the awesome presence of the Lord. The void that was in us before vanished! We call that week **"the week that changed our lives forever."** For months after the week of our encounter with God, the anointing was tangible in our bodies. Even today, when the Holy Spirit moves in meetings, we sense His presence in us in a tangible way. It took an encounter with God to set our lives on a new course to pursue God's will for us. That encounter brought us to the mission field. Through that encounter, we learned to recognize the voice of the Lord. That encounter increased our hunger for Him. I can go on and on. If it was not for that encounter, we would not make it in the ministry. That encounter paved the way for many other encounters with God. Every one has been different, yet similar. Different on the outside and similar on the inside.

Friend, the most important thing I have learned through this encounter with God is that everyone needs to be supernaturally touched by the Living God. Such an encounter with God will thrust you into a realm where God is so real all else disappears before Him. A realm filled with wonder, awe, and power; where the fear of God brings you to your knees. It will thrust you into God's direction and will for your life. You need it as deeply as I need it—just like you need water to live and oxygen to breathe.

Do not be satisfied with a one-time deal with God that happened somewhere in the distant past. Make it your mission in life to be a prime candidate to experience a touch from heaven not once, not twice, but many times—over and over again. But remember, it all starts with sacrifice. What do you have prepared for God to touch in your life? Gideon prepared a meal that cost him much. Are you willing to pay the price?

Another thing I want us to look at in this chapter is the fact that the Angel vanished after He touched the sacrifice. He vanished, but He was as close as ever! He once again became the Unseen One.

Look Behind the Curtain

One day, while visiting family in South Africa, I took time to play with my brother's children. One was five years old and the other three years old at the time. We played hide and seek. We had so much fun! They would run into a room to hide from me and I would come looking for them. Well, it was always easy to find them because they did not spend much time to look for a good place to hide. The thrill of being found was too great. One time I went to hide from them. I stood behind the curtain in a place in the room where I could see them but they could not see me. I watched them very closely. They came running into the room with much excitement—brimming with joy, even—stirring up a great noise. After the initial entrance, their faces changed. The excitement that rushed in with them left them all alone in the big room. Their faces said it all: "He must be here, he came into this room, but now he is gone." The three-year-old lost interest quickly. He saw something else on the bed. The five-year-old was so disappointed that I was "gone," she began to cry. If only she knew I was very close, indeed. I could just reach out my hand and touch her. Oh, what joy when they found out I was right there in that "empty" room! Friend, how is it that so many of us are like those two kids? We follow God into a situation of life, and when, at first, we do not see Him or hear from Him, we lose interest. We either get busy with something else, or we are so disappointed that we are filled with despair and resentment toward God. Remember, just because we feel we are alone does not mean we are. Just because we think we are alone we are not. Just because you do not have a sense of God's presence on a given moment does not mean that He is somewhere else, doing something else.

Vanished?

Many times after an encounter with God, after the goosebumps and excitement of the awesome moments in the manifest power of the Lord, He "vanishes"! The anointing lifts from you. Many preachers will tell you that Monday morning, after a great Sunday's meetings, is often challenging. It was to me. In the beginning, I could not understand how I could feel the presence of Almighty God and how I could flow in the anointing on Sunday, and then the very next day be down in the dumps! The Lord gave me the answer, as always: "My son, I am as real on Monday as on any other day of the week. In the realm of the natural, it might seem to you I appear and disappear, but I am in Reality always present." The problem with so many of us is that we jump from reality to reality, realm to realm, and situation to situation. God wants us to be stuck in one place: the Divine Reality! Since this broke through in my spirit, I can actually look forward to Monday! Yes, I still do have my off moments, but not for long.

Too many of God's people live from experience to experience. Keep in mind, our whole lives are an experience with the Lord. Gideon had his experience and now it was time to act. Everything the Lord does has a purpose! Let me say this again: The Lord does not touch us just to let us know He is

God and we are not! He does not need to prove His Lordship. He is God, whether we believe it or not. Every miracle, every word, and every encounter is a commission to act. Someone once said, "Don't show me a man who received ten words from the Lord and seeks another. Rather, show me a man with just one word, obediently acting on that word."

Evan Roberts, the humble man that God used so mightily to change a nation during the revival in Wales, said: *"Only the man who lives in fellowship with Divine Reality can be used to call the people to God."* Once you find your place in the Divine Reality, God wants to draw others into the same place in Him, through you! God's people are drawn into the Divine Reality. But before you find your place in the Divine Reality, you have to enter into that Reality. Most often, a touch of God is the door!

Food for Thought:

- An encounter with the Living God will change your life.

- You can encounter God.

- God wants to touch others through you.

Opened Eyes See Better!

A nd when Gideon perceived that He was the Angel of the Lord, Gideon said, "Alas, O Lord God! For now I have seen the Angel of the Lord face to face!" (Judges 6:22).

In the previous chapter, we looked at the importance of an encounter with God and the many great things that can happen to you when you encounter God. In this chapter, we will look at one of them: Your eyes will be opened to the Divine Reality.

"If you see God face to face you will die!" This is an ancient superstition that found its way through the corridors of time right into the lives of many present-day believers. It was formed way before the time of Gideon and he believed it with

75

all his heart. I have read this verse many times through the glasses of this superstition and thought it to be true, until the Lord revealed it to me as a fallacy. If you believe no man can see the Lord face-to-face and live to tell about it, you will interpret verse 22 something like this: When Gideon saw the Person he was speaking to all this time was actually *God*, He was filled with a fear that he was going to die. One can picture him standing there, in the winepress, looking up anxiously for a thunderstorm; afraid to be zapped by God. Such an interpretation would only satisfy about half of my heart. I believe there is another revelation here in these words. Let me explain.

God appears to different people 44 times in the Bible. Nowhere in the Bible is there an account of someone who died during or right after one of these appearances. These appearances were very real and face-to-face. We read in Exodus 33:11, ...*the Lord spoke to Moses face to face, as a man speaks to his friend.* There are many in the Bible who had similar encounters: Abraham, Isaac, Jacob, Gideon, John, and Paul, among others. Not one of them died because they saw God, but each of them actually benefited greatly. They were touched and blessed and their lives were thrust into a higher dimension of living!

Paul saw the Lord in His Glory on the road to Damascus. Acts 9:3-4 says:

> *As he traveled on, he came near to Damascus, and suddenly a light from heaven flashed around him, and he fell to the ground. Then he heard a voice saying to him, "Saul, Saul, why are you persecuting Me?"*

The awesome power of the Light he saw blinded his eyes! He saw the Light of God and could not see anything else for three days. Even after three days Ananias had to pray for him about his sight and after that prayer something fell from

Saul's (Paul's) eyes like scales (verse 18). How great is the power of the Glory of the Lord that it can blind you for three days and you need a miracle to see again? This makes me think of a song we used to sing often: *"Turn your eyes upon Jesus, Look full in His wonderful face. And the things of earth will grow strangely dim, in the light of His Glory and grace."* Paul experienced first-hand the reality of this song.

Now this same Paul writes in 1 Timothy 6:16 about the Lord:

> *Who alone has immortality... and lives in unapproachable light, Whom no man has ever seen or can see. Unto Him be honor and everlasting power and dominion. Amen.*

The Lord is unapproachable in the Light within which He lives. It is impossible to approach Him in the natural. The Glory of the Lord is not a cloud or even a light. God hides Himself in a cloud or a bright light so man can live to tell of the encounter. The Glory of the Lord is all that makes God, God—nothing is held back! Paul never saw the Lord Jesus in the natural, as He taught on the mountain. He never saw the Lord physically as He raised the dead, healed the sick, and fed the multitudes, but he saw the Lord in His Glory and that changed his life. His encounter was so real it consumed him from that day on. He was instantly turned and persuaded about which direction he needed to take. His heart was so transformed by this encounter that, through the inspiration of the Holy Spirit, he wrote most of the New Testament as we know it. He did not die when he saw God, but he truly *lived*! Our physical bodies cannot function properly in the realm of the Glory of God. Paul was blinded. Others could not stand before the Lord. Their strength left their bodies like the priests at the dedication of the temple (2 Chronicles 5:14).

Paul writes that our bodies will be transformed when we go to be with Jesus. We will receive a glorified body, much like Jesus did when He was resurrected. This glorified body will enable us to function in heaven (1 Corinthians 15).

John, on the Island of Patmos, saw the Lord in His Glory. The glory was so great that his natural body could not take it. Revelation 1:17 says, *When I saw Him, I fell at His feet as if dead.* He did not die, even though his body wanted to. John became alive! Yes, he was on an island, deserted and left to die. He did not have much going for him, until he saw the Lord. In this encounter, the Lord showed him things so dramatic and real that even today we have a hard time understanding it all. Wow! The same John who wrote in his account of the Gospel: *No man has ever seen God at any time* (John 1:18). According to historians, he wrote the gospel around 90 A.D. and had this encounter with God around 96 A.D. John was the beloved disciple of Jesus. He was in the inner circle of Jesus and walked and talked with Jesus for over three years. Yet, the most defining day of his life was on Patmos when He saw the Lord in Resurrection Glory! First, the Lord revealed Himself to John through Jesus, His Son, in the realm of the natural. Then He stepped up the power, "added" His Glory to the encounter, and thrust John into another realm: the Divine Reality!

Do You Want to See Jesus?

In meetings, when I ask people if they want to see Jesus, virtually all respond with a definite "Yes." Oh, to see Him and look upon His face! "How we long to see Him," they say. The fact is, many expect Him to be a little baby in a manger. Others expect Him to be a gentle shepherd with a lamb in his arms. Some think they will see Him hanging on a cross, or speaking to some poor sufferer of an incurable sickness. Friend, I want to see Him the way Moses saw Him. Moses had to hide his face so all of Israel would not be scared out of their minds. I want to see Him in the Light of His Glory, like Paul, who was blinded for three days from the distractions of the world. I want to join John on the ground as a dead man the moment Jesus appears in full resurrection power. I want to see Jesus on the throne in heaven, a scepter in His hands, high and lifted up! I want to see the flame of fire in His eyes. Are you scared you will die when that happens? No—I am scared that I will not really live if it does not happen—if I die in the process, I will be where every Christian wants to be: with Jesus Christ.

It can be said that no one has ever seen the Lord, Complete and Glorious, without anything held back. Moses came very close. He saw the backward parts of the Lord and even then he had to be protected in the cleft of the rock (Exodus 33:18-23). Paul writes about us:

And all of us, as with unveiled face, [because we] continued to behold [in the Word of God] as in a mirror the glory of the Lord, are constantly being transfigured into His very own image in ever increasing splendor and from one degree of glory to another; [for this comes] from the Lord [Who is] the Spirit (2 Corinthians 3:18).

As we see the Lord and encounter Him in our lives, layer by layer of the protective light that surrounds Him is stripped away and we are changed to be like Him. There is something that is brighter than the brightest light; that makes the sun, moon, and stars to lose their shine and be darkened (Isaiah 13:9-10). It is God's Glory. It overpowers everything! Isaiah 2:19 says the people shall

...go into the caves of the rocks and into the holes of the earth from before the terror and dread of the Lord and from before the glory of His majesty, when He arises to shake mightily and terribly the earth.

Gideon's eyes were opened. He perceived that it was the Angel of the Lord he was talking with all along. If that was me, by now I would have started to kick myself. There I was, all the time, talking with the Living God, Creator of all things! What did I talk about? I complained about some stupid enemy making my life miserable. I reasoned with Him and questioned every answer and statement He made as if I knew better! I had the opportunity to ask any important question I have ever wondered about and He would probably have given me the answer to it, but I did not ask. I had the unique opportunity to join the angels of heaven and bow my knee before the Almighty and worship at His feet, but I did not. Is not that reason enough to throw your hands in the air and cry out, *"Alas, O Lord God!"*? The Hebrew word for Alas is *Ahahh* which is an exclamation of pain. The pain came from his heart and not his body. For a brief moment, Gideon cried out in pain, looking at the wasted opportunity. Yes, there was a wasted opportunity, but at least his eyes were opened now!

He received new vision with his new commission. He could see things hidden from him before. He now had a vision of the Divine Reality imprinted in his spirit. He gained access to a higher life.

A New Adventure

Through the whole of 1995, the Lord prompted us to follow Him to new places. Places He would show us and take us to. He started to gently and slowly release us from our loving church and friends and all our securities. We knew He was doing it and we enjoyed seeing Him at work in our lives, even though the work He was doing at the time did not always bring comfort to us. We knew we needed to make more decisions and commitments that were not going to be easy to make. We faced a major uprooting from a country and life we loved, traveling 8,000 miles across the Atlantic ocean without securities, families, or familiarities, learning a new culture and living in a foreign country—all based on our faith in God!

One night, after Sharon and I came from a revival meeting in Johannesburg, South Africa, we were sleeping in my parent's home in Witfield. In the early morning hours, I had a dream. It was so real that I have to say, like Paul, *Whether* [it was] *in the body or out of the body I do not know, God knows* (2 Corinthians 12:2). I dreamed I was in a large church building. The church was empty. I was walking along one of the walls toward the back of the building when suddenly the door right in front of me burst open and a whirlwind blew into the sanctuary. At first, it startled me and I ran toward the windows screaming, "The blinds, the blinds!" I was afraid that the wind would cause damage to the blinds that covered the windows. As I watched the wind blow past the blinds, I realized that the blinds were not affected by this powerful wind at all. They were just hanging still as if there was no violent whirlwind blowing through the church. Only then did I realize this was no ordinary wind. I remember starting to walk backwards away from this wind, without taking my eyes off it. Suddenly, the wind changed into a blinding light, right before my eyes, and it started to pick up speed as it moved along the wall away from me. I was filled with a Divine Fear and knew it was the Holy Spirit. I sensed the Presence of the Lord filling the building. Just thinking of it stirs my heart again. The Light suddenly changed direction and sped toward the front of the huge sanctuary at an ever-increasing speed. Then the Light changed direction again, this time coming right toward me. I tried to put more distance between us, but knew it was no use. With such speed as I have never seen before the Light hit me in the center of my breastbone! I was knocked off my feet, but the force of the "collision" lifted me **up** to the high ceiling of the church. I was in no pain and felt a perfect peace. I remember drifting downward, like a feather, until I reached the ground. At that moment I woke up, trembling with the power of God. For several hours, until the anointing started to lift from me, I could not move in my bed as the power of the Lord surged through my body.

I had an encounter with God again! He showed the direction to take for our lives without saying a word. Somehow He told me without saying it—I just knew. We were on our way to America, following the Lord where He was leading us. Interestingly enough, Sharon had exactly the same dream two weeks later, with the same experience of peace and power. Our God is truly an awesome God! He opened our eyes to see His Glorious Light wherever we might go. He sharpened His vision in us and set us in the Divine Reality.

What Do You See?

Too many people go through life with eyes that do not see, facing life's trials and difficulties without perception of the Great Living God Who, although He sometimes seems to have vanished, is always close by. Once your eyes are opened, you will and can never be the same again. If He brought Gideon out of the winepress, if He took Paul—who intended to destroy God's precious work—off the road to Damascus, if He picked John off an island of desolation and complete isolation into the realm of heaven, where he gained so much height he saw the future unfolding before his eyes, if He carried these two simple South Africans half way across the world to do God's work—just think what He can do for you! You do not have to go through life solely relying on your natural eyes for vision. The Lord wants to open, deep in your spirit, a pair of spiritual eyes which, with a little practice, some more determination, and total consecration, will become your primary source for vision and perception.

The Lord asked Jeremiah: *"What do you see?"* (Jeremiah. 1:11). He asked Amos: *"What do you see?"* (Amos 7:8). He asked Zechariah: *"What do you see?"* (Zechariah. 4:2). Every one of these prophets saw something the Lord revealed to them. Jeremiah started out seeing the branch of an almond tree, in a simple, yet powerful, vision. The almond tree is always first to blossom when spring is approaching. It is first to show signs of life after the winter. In Jeremiah 1:12, we read: *You have seen well, for I am alert and active, watching over My word to perform it.* All of Israel had been in a season of winter. Although there were periods of revival on the political and religious front, as a whole, this was a season of sin and pride in Israel. God told Jeremiah He would quickly fulfill His promises in Jeremiah's life. Signs of new life would come forth soon! God was about to bring Israel back to Him, even if it meant destroying the temple and Jerusalem. God, as always, was more concerned with their hearts than with their comfort. God is asking you today: *"What do you see?"* Sometimes I wonder whether we are seeing anything at all. Our prayer every day should be, "Lord open my spirit eyes so I can truly see."

Food for Thought:

- Seeing God will thrust you into a higher dimension of living.
- Spiritual Eyesight does not come naturally; it comes through spiritual exercise.
- Opened eyes see better.

Sacred Peace

*T*he Lord said to him, "Peace be to you, do not fear; you shall not die" (Judges 6:23).

"I am immortal until I have fulfilled God's purpose for my life." What a powerful statement made by a precious man of God in Cali, Colombia. This pastor received numerous threats, including ones against his life, as he and his family labored in the Kingdom of God in Cali, a city infested with all the evil revolving around a multi-million dollar drug-smuggling business. At first he was concerned for his life, but after a time of fasting and prayer, a supernatural peace came over him. He uttered the above statement many times. He prayed continuously for revival to overtake Cali. All the pastors in the region drew strength from this humble yet strong man of God. One day, while going to a pastor's meeting, he was gunned down and died on the sidewalk near the entrance to a church. The entire church community was shocked by his tragic death, but the Lord gave his family the same supernatural peace. At his funeral, the pastors of Cali made a vow of unity and it resulted in the transformation of the whole city. The once-powerful druglords were all arrested and people started to turn back to the Lord. One of the most intriguing and compelling facts about this true story is the power of the peace the Lord can give a person.

Peace When Things Do Not Make Sense

If you read through the Bible, you find countless examples of the amazing, wonderful peace of God in the lives of His people—especially when trouble was on the horizon of their lives. Think of Daniel and how he continued to pray to God—even when he knew it would mean becoming "dinner" to starved lions. Think about his three friends who, facing death in a furnace of fire, were calm, cool, and collected before the powerful king. Think of Stephen, standing in a shower of stones and rocks, looking into the heavens with the peace of God upon him, seeing the Glory of the Lord. Think of Christians who faced hungry lions, sharpened swords, ropes of pain, and the hatred of many, only to be unmoved by circumstance—with hearts full of forgiveness even to those who harmed them. Think of Jesus, hanging on the cross in agony and pain. How He had to exercise complete self-control not to call legions of angels at His disposal to rescue Him. How He hung there all alone, looked mankind in the eye, and said with loving words, "Father, forgive them, for they know not what they have done." Think of Rachel Scott, trapped inside her school in Littleton, Colorado, staring death in the face. How she responded when one of the gunmen asked her: "Do you believe in God?" She could have said no and lived, but rather she said, "Yes, I believe in God." She was gunned down and now she really lives.

The list goes on and on. What enables the people of God to respond in these "unnatural" ways? The answer, my friend, is the peace of God. Paul writes about this special peace:

> *And God's peace [shall be yours, that tranquil state of a soul assured of its salvation through Christ, and so fearing nothing from God and being content with its earthly lot of whatever sort that is, that peace] which transcends all understanding shall garrison and mount guard over your hearts and minds in Christ Jesus* (Philippians 4:7).

The Hebrew word for peace is *Shalom*. The Jewish community today still uses this word as a greeting. Instead of "Hello" or "Goodbye,"they say, *Shalom*. Strong's concordance lists all that *Shalom* is: **safe, i.e. (fig.) well, happy, friendly; also (abstr.) welfare, i.e. health, prosperity, peace, (good) health, perfect peace (-able, -ably), prosper (-ity, -ous), rest, safe (-ly), salute, welfare, all is well, wholly.**

The *Shalom* of God makes a person complete. Complete in health. Complete in safety. Complete in happiness. Complete in prosperity. Complete in rest. *Shalom* is the absence of sickness, fear, doubt, and danger. *Shalom* brings wholeness to you. It puts the broken pieces of your life together again. This is very important. Without peace, you will not be able to do what God wants you to do. You will soon worry about how to do it, or fear failure. You will look at yourself and see all your shortcomings. When peace floods your soul, you will be at rest with yourself, knowing God will do what He said He will do.

Gideon received Divine peace and it drove out his fear. No time to die now, Gideon, there is work to do! God's peace became the legacy of Gideon's encounter with God. It thrust him out of the winepress into the battlefield; out of hiding into pursuit.

Someone once told me, "Rudi, never make an important decision in the absence of the peace of God. Let peace be your referee in life!" A pastor in South Africa was mightily used of God to give Divine counsel to people, especially when they faced important decisions. People would come and ask him which direction to take. "Should I buy that property?" "Should I apply for that job?" He would pray and the Lord would answer him with direction to give to the people. One day, someone asked him the secret of hearing God's voice for specific situations. He said he would take the question at hand and look at all the possible answers. He would then pray about every answer individually. The moment the peace of God rushed through his soul, he would stop. That would be God's answer! He was always led by God's peace in his heart. God's peace will give you full assurance that what you are about to do is the will of God and it will turn out right. My prayer for you is that you will find that peace in your situation. Peace be with you!

The very moment the peace of God flooded his soul, Gideon worshiped God by building an altar. He called it "The Lord is Peace." Every issue in his life was settled! All the turmoil, fear, and anguish that had raged through his soul like a great storm disappeared before the peace of the Lord. The fact is, you can have the same peace flowing through your soul. The Prince of Peace (Jesus) is with you right now to take command over your storm, your pain, your turmoil, your fear, your life!

Gideon's life was changed. He would never be the same again. He began a new walk with God. He came out of hiding, fear, humiliation. He came out of the winepress. He stopped beating wheat in the wrong place. He exchanged his tools for weapons, his cloak for armor, his self-pity for courage, the reality of his situation for the Divine Reality. He started living in the realm of God and immediately he started to see miracles, wonders, signs, favor, boldness, victory—things he only dreamed of before. When fear came knocking, God lifted him higher and higher and higher into the Divine Reality.

Friend, today can be the beginning of a new life in God for you! You can experience the same changes Gideon did. The higher life in the Divine Reality is within your grasp. Why not live it? My prayer for you is that this book will thrust you into the road, out of hiding into living—*true living!* Stop the life of mere existence and start the exploits God has planned for you!

Food for Thought:

- Peace makes you complete.
- Peace is your referee in life.
- Trade your hiding place for the Secret Place of the Most High.

For more information on the ministry of
Rudi and Sharon Swanepoel, write to:

God's Glory Ministries International
PO Box 1222
Elyria OH 44036

or visit them on the Web at
<u>www.godsglory.org</u>

You can also visit their church:

First Assembly of God
525 N. Abbe Rd.
Elyria OH 44035

Tel: **(440) 366-8871**

Fax: **(440) 365-8720**